Date: 7/27/16

21st
Century
Skills Library

ROAD TO RECOVERY

FLORIDA PANTHER

Barbara A. Somervill

Cherry Lake Publishing
Ann Arbor, Michigan

CHERRY
LAKE
Publishing

Published in the United States of America by Cherry Lake Publishing
Ann Arbor, Michigan
www.cherrylakepublishing.com

Content Adviser: Stephen L. Williams, President and Founder, Florida Panther
Society, Inc., Gainesville, Florida

Photo Credits: Cover and page 12, ©Photo courtesy of U.S. Fish and Wildlife Service;
page 4, ©M. Timothy O'Keefe/Alamy; page 7, ©Mark J. Barrett/Alamy; page 9, ©Bruce
Coleman, Inc./Alamy; page 10, ©Purestock/Alamy; page 14, ©Kelly Braden/Alamy;
page 17, ©iStockphoto.com/johnandersonphoto; page 18, ©SCPhotos/Alamy; page 20,
©AP Photo/Gregory Smith; page 22, ©AP Photo/Lynne Sladky; page 25, ©iStockphoto.
com/anniam

Map by XNR Productions Inc.

Library of Congress Cataloging-in-Publication Data
Somervill, Barbara A.
Florida panther / Barbara A. Somervill.
    p. cm.—(Road to recovery)
ISBN-13: 978-1-60279-316-3
ISBN-10: 1-60279-316-6
1. Florida panther—Juvenile literature. I. Title. II. Series.
QL737.C23S5835 2009
599.75'24—dc22   2008024227

Cherry Lake Publishing would like to acknowledge the work of
The Partnership for 21st Century Skills.
Please visit www.21stcenturyskills.org for more information.

TABLE OF CONTENTS

CHAPTER ONE
In the Everglades   4

CHAPTER TWO
The Story of Florida Panthers   9

CHAPTER THREE
Endangered!   14

CHAPTER FOUR
The Road to Recovery   20

CHAPTER FIVE
Florida Panthers Today   25

Map   29

Glossary   30

For More Information   31

Index   32

About the Author   32

IN THE EVERGLADES

A Florida panther grooms its fur. Panthers spend much of the day resting.

A female Florida panther lies sleeping on her side. Her two young kittens lie next to her. They are just a few days old. The kittens have speckled fur, and their tails have five dark rings. Their blue eyes haven't opened yet. Each kitten weighs a little more than 1 pound (454 grams) now, but will grow quickly. Their mother's milk is very rich. It contains six times more fat than cow's milk. A steady milk diet will help the kittens gain weight. They will weigh about 9 pounds (4 kilograms) in just 2 months.

The female panther lives deep in the Florida Everglades. Her home territory measures just 75 square miles (194 square kilometers). Luckily, she is a skilled hunter. While she nurses her kittens, she can eat much more than the usual panther diet of 20 to 30 pounds (9 to 14 kg) of meat at a time.

At dusk, the female leaves her kittens alone in the den. She is hungry and must hunt to keep up her milk supply.

21st Century Content

The Everglades is a wetland that once covered most of southern Florida. In the past 100 years, increased human demands for land and water have reduced the size of the Everglades by half. This loss of land affects the plants and animals that live in the wetlands. Fourteen endangered **species**, including manatees, leatherback and green turtles, wood storks, and snail kites, reside in the Everglades. What should be done to protect the Everglades? Do you think that the government should pass strict laws to protect the endangered species?

White-tailed deer, wild hogs, and raccoons live within the panther's home range. This evening she will feed on wild hog. It is protein-rich, fatty, and **nutritious**.

The panther kittens will stay with their mother for up to 2 years. The exact amount of time varies. The kittens usually remain in the den for the first 2 months. During that time, they drink only mother's milk. When they are about 8 weeks old, they join their mother when she hunts. They also begin eating meat. The kittens continue to grow and change. By 6 months, they lose their spots and tail rings. They are the same brown color as adult panthers. Their eyes change from blue to golden brown. By the time they

The spots on a panther kitten's fur help it blend in with its surroundings.

are 1 year old, the kittens can catch small prey such as rabbits and wood rats. Over time, their hunting skills improve. They will be able to hunt larger animals such as raccoons and armadillos. When they grow large enough, the young panthers will be able to bring down a wild hog or a deer.

When the panthers are about 2 years old, they leave their mother. The young female panther may settle in a new range that overlaps her mother's territory. The young male faces a more difficult life. Other adult males will challenge him and force him farther from home. He will have to establish his own home range. To do that, he will probably have to fight other males to gain territory and mating rights.

The mother and her kittens are a critical part of the survival story of Florida panthers in the wild. Three panthers make a difference. There are fewer than 75 Florida panthers in existence. Every panther counts.

CHAPTER TWO

THE STORY OF FLORIDA PANTHERS

Florida panthers are built for hunting. They can run as fast as 35 miles (56 kilometers) per hour for short distances.

Florida panthers are members of a large-cat family called *Puma concolor*. Their relatives include mountain lions, cougars, and pumas. The family includes 30 **subspecies**. Its members are scattered across North America, Central America, and South America. The Florida panther is

Florida panthers have very sharp teeth. Even their tongues have sharp points that help remove meat from prey.

confined to a small region of southern Florida. It is smaller than its cousins. Panthers have longer legs, smaller feet, and shorter, reddish-brown fur than other members of the cougar family.

Florida panthers, *Puma concolor coryi,* measure about 24 inches (61 centimeters) at the shoulder. Males are normally larger than females. Adult males weigh between

100 and 155 pounds (45 and 70 kg). They measure about 6 to 8 feet (1.8 to 2.4 meters) from their noses to the tips of their tails. Females usually weigh between 66 and 100 pounds (30 and 45 kg) and measure 5 to 7 feet (1.5 to 2.1 m) long.

All cats are **carnivores**. Big cats, such as panthers, are usually the top **predators** in their regions. They have no true natural predators. Panthers, however, prey on several species. Ninety percent of a panther's diet is made up of wild hogs, white-tailed deer, armadillos, and raccoons. But panthers will also eat wood rats, rabbits, and a variety of wading birds.

An adult panther eats one deer or hog each week. Raccoons and armadillos provide far less food value. A panther would need to eat ten raccoons to equal the food available in one deer. Panthers eat until they are full and then hide their catch under leaves and twigs.

Florida Fish and Wildlife Service workers take care of a tranquilized panther. Veterinarians and other workers help keep panthers healthy.

Panthers can live to be 10 to 15 years old in the wild. But males often live fewer years because they fight for territory. Repeated battles will decrease a panther's lifespan.

Other dangers for the big cats are diseases. Some develop infections in wounds. Others get diseases such as rabies or feline leukemia. Scientists use tranquilizer darts to capture panthers and treat them with **vaccines** to prevent such diseases. They put radio collars on the panthers to monitor their movements.

Many panthers also die or are seriously injured when they try to cross highways and are struck by vehicles. Twenty-five panthers died from vehicle collisions between 1978 and 1999. This may seem like a low number of deaths, but it is far more than the small Florida panther population can stand.

Learning & Innovation Skills

Sometimes problem solving means finding new uses for old ideas. For example, to keep humans safe when crossing busy roads, engineers designed overhead and underground walkways. In 1993, conservationists decided to build underpasses for panthers and other wildlife along highway I-75 in southern Florida. Building underpasses is just one safety method that has been adapted to help protect panthers and other animals.

CHAPTER THREE

ENDANGERED!

A panther's eyes allow it to see well at night.

Once Florida panthers roamed as far west as Louisiana and as far north as southern Tennessee. They ranged from the Mississippi River east to the Atlantic Ocean. The subspecies is now limited to four counties in southern Florida. Florida panthers are one of the most endangered subspecies in the world.

Before Europeans arrived in southeastern North America, Native Americans and panthers lived on the same land. The Cherokee called the panther *Klandagi,* or "lord of the forest." For the Chickasaw, the panther was *Ko-icto,* "cat of god." The big cat was respected by native people and appears in much of their folklore. The Seminoles taught their children to be quiet at sunset, the time when panthers hunt. The people believed that if the panther lost its prey, the village would suffer some form of sickness.

The arrival of Europeans changed the future of panthers. Early pioneers believed that panthers were a danger to humans and livestock. They worried that panthers would kill too many of the game animals that the settlers depended on for food. Settlers felt threatened by the panthers and responded by killing them. Although the slaughter of Florida panthers began in the 1600s, it

continued well into the 20th century. In 1887, the government of Florida began paying hunters $5 for every panther they killed.

It wasn't until 1950 that the Florida Game and Freshwater Fish Commission restricted hunting panthers to deer season. Eight years later, the commission made hunting panthers illegal. But it was already too late. More than 300 years of killing had nearly wiped out the population of Florida panthers. In 1967, the panther was officially listed as **endangered**. Only about 30 Florida panthers existed at that time.

In the past 40 years, Florida's human population has exploded. In 1970, the

Thousands of acres of Everglades wetlands have been lost to development and agriculture. Human activities have had a big impact on panthers and other wildlife.

state's population was about 7 million people. By 2000, the number exceeded 15 million. It is estimated that Florida's population will be close to 30 million by 2030.

People have spread into areas once occupied only by wildlife. **Developers** drain wetlands and build houses, roads, and businesses. In south Florida, more than 1,000 acres (405 hectares) of wetland is filled in each year.

A Florida panther kitten rests in some brush. Human activity has greatly reduced the amount of habitat available for panthers.

All of this development has a big effect on water resources. Building canals changes the flow of water. Habitat loss and changes in water flow create serious problems for panther survival.

The loss and **fragmentation** of habitat have created another problem—a small **gene** pool. Healthy animal populations have wide gene pools. This means that there are a large number of other animals available to mate with. A large number of mates provides **genetic diversity**. For Florida panthers, there are few other animals to mate with. There is little genetic diversity in their populations. Mating is limited to a very small group. In the past 40 years, scientists have begun to see genetic problems in panther young. Many panthers now have crooks in their tails and cowlicks in their hair. A more serious problem is that the number of successful births is lower and some kittens are born with defective hearts. If panthers are to survive in the wild, something must be done to help make sure that kittens will be born healthy.

CHAPTER FOUR

THE ROAD TO RECOVERY

*A panther is released in Big Cypress National Preserve. It
wears a radio collar that helps experts track it.*

Saving the Florida panther requires a Species Survival

Plan. Every endangered species has a survival plan. It

outlines the goals that conservationists hope to reach.

The first Florida panther survival plan was presented in 1981. The plan is updated periodically.

The goal is to have 3 to 4 separate populations with at least 240 Florida panthers in each population. To consider the plan a success, the populations will have to survive on their own for 14 years. To achieve this goal, there will need to be enough habitat to support these populations. It will not be easy.

In 1974, the U.S. Congress approved the formation of Big Cypress National Preserve in southern Florida. The state of Florida purchased another panther habitat, called the Fakahatchee Strand State Preserve. In 1989, the Florida Panther National Wildlife Refuge was established. This was a good start. Still, all three pieces of land put together provided only enough land for one panther population. Land in Florida—even swampland—is very expensive. Conservation groups have difficulty purchasing and

Experts can recognize Florida panther tracks. Scientists will continue to closely monitor panther activity and behavior in the years to come.

maintaining enough habitat. Land is in high demand. Developers often pressure government leaders to let them use land that has been set aside for wildlife.

The current survival plan calls for moving some panthers to other places where Florida panthers lived in the past. Possible reintroduction sites are in northern Florida, Georgia, Alabama, and Arkansas. This idea isn't popular with some of the people who live in those places. The amount of land required to support 240 panthers is large—thousands of square miles or kilometers. It will take a lot of land to support the 3 or 4 populations of at least 240 panthers needed to ensure their survival.

Many people fear having predators in their neighborhood. There is no official record of a Florida panther ever attacking a human, but that does not stop the fear. Some people are more concerned for their pets than for themselves. This concern is real. Hungry panthers are known to kill cats and dogs for food. In addition, some people who like to hunt deer and wild hogs don't want to compete with panthers for game animals.

Efforts to improve the Florida panther gene pool have had mixed results. **Captive breeding** was attempted in

the early 1990s. It failed because it took too long to get approval for the plan. By the time the plan was approved, the captive females were too old to produce young. This was a tragedy. Females that might have had kittens in the wild were prevented from doing so. Their important breeding years went to waste because of poor planning.

Another idea to improve the panther gene pool is to introduce Texas cougars into it. Texas cougars are close relatives and can breed with Florida panthers. Scientists hope that breeding Florida panthers with Texas cougars will reduce birth defects in panther newborns and produce a healthier panther population.

FLORIDA PANTHERS TODAY

Panther crossing signs are used on some Florida highways to help keep panthers safe.

Progress is being made in the fight to save the Florida panther from **extinction**. But we still don't know if that progress is enough. In 2007, it was estimated that between 80 and 100 panthers lived in southern Florida. That is more than double the number that lived there

in the early 1950s. These numbers are encouraging, but there are still too few panthers for long-term survival.

In the past 50 years, scientists have identified the problems that exist for panthers. They have worked to reduce the effects of those problems. Panther habitat has been placed in federal or state hands and protected. Education programs teach the public about the panther's needs. A 42-member Recovery Team watches out for the panther's interests.

Keeping Florida panthers alive and healthy is a top priority for people working to save the panthers. Disease is a serious concern. Wild panthers get diseases from other animals and carry them into their population. A program is reducing the impact of disease on panthers. Every time scientists give shots to panthers to reduce disease, they also put radio collars on the animals. Scientists can learn a lot about panther behavior by studying where and when panthers move.

Twenty-four wildlife crossings have been built along the stretch of road called Alligator Alley. This road runs through the Everglades from Florida's west coast to its east coast. Unfortunately, these crossings haven't solved the problem of panthers being hit by cars. The first 6 months of 2007 saw 14 deaths. That was 3 more than the 11 deaths recorded in 2006. Conservationists are studying

Living with panthers is possible. A brochure called "A Guide to Living with Florida Panthers" explains how humans can adapt to sharing territory with the big cats. People in Florida panther territory should protect their pets and livestock with electrified fences. Outdoor lights and motion sensors can reduce panther interest in a backyard. If a panther becomes a nuisance, residents should call the local wildlife agency and have it moved. Developing habits that allow humans and panthers to live together peacefully is just one way to help panthers survive.

where the deaths take place. They are trying to find solutions to the problem.

Helping panthers survive is becoming more difficult as more people move into Florida. Some people think that we should just let the species die out. Then more land would be available for planting sugarcane, citrus orchards, or fields of vegetables. But getting rid of the panthers would create other problems. The populations of white-tailed deer, wild hogs, raccoons, and other animals would increase. Eventually there would be too many of those animals and not enough food to go around. Then many deer, hogs, raccoons and other animals would be lost to starvation and disease.

Nature provides a balance between meat-eaters and plant-eaters. Florida panthers are part of that balance. They are the state mammal and the state's largest predator. Florida's leaders must decide what steps they are willing to take to save the panthers.

UNITED STATES

area of map

ATLANTIC
OCEAN

Florida

Gulf of Mexico

N
W   E
S

0   100 mi
0   100 km

Current range of the Florida panther

This map shows the current range of Florida panthers.

Glossary

captive breeding (KAP-tihv BREE-ding) a breeding program to produce young in zoos or other nature preserves

carnivores (KAR-nuh-vorz) animals or plants that eat meat

developers (dih-VEL-uh-purz) people who buy land and make it usable for building homes, stores, or offices

endangered (en-DAYN-jurd) in danger of dying out completely

extinction (ek-STINGK-shuhn) no longer having any living members of a species

fragmentation (frag-muhn-TAY-shuhn) the breaking up or separation of a habitat or wilderness area

gene (JEEN) a part of a cell; traits such as eye color are passed on from parent to child through genes

genetic diversity (juh-NET-ik di-VUR-suh-tee) having a wide range and variation of genes within a species

habitat (HAB-uh-tat) the place where an animal or plant naturally lives and grows

nutritious (noo-TRISH-uhss) providing food value to make an animal or plant healthy

predators (PREH-duh-turz) animals that hunt and eat other animals

species (SPEE-sheez) a group of similar plants or animals

subspecies (SUB-spee-sheez) a smaller group within a species

vaccines (VAK-seenz) medicines that prevent disease

FOR MORE INFORMATION

Books

Ake, Anne. *Everglades: An Ecosystem Facing Choices and Challenges*. Sarasota, FL: Pineapple Press, 2008.

Caper, William. *Florida Panthers: Struggle for Survival*. New York: Bearport Publishing, 2008.

Godown, Jan. *Florida's Famous Animals: True Stories of Sunset Sam the Dolphin, Snooty the Manatee, Big Guy the Panther, and Others*. Guildford, CT: Globe Pequot Press, 2008.

Web Sites

Florida Panther Net—Official Education Site
www.floridaconservation.org/panther/
The official Florida Panther Web site developed by the Florida
Fish and Wildlife Conservation Commission

Help Save the Endangered Florida Panther
floridapanther.org/
Information about what people are doing to help save Florida panthers

Florida Everglades
www.cotf.edu/ete/modules/everglades/FEpanther.html
To learn more about the Florida Everglades habitat that is home to Florida panthers

INDEX

Big Cypress National
    Preserve, 21
birth defects, 19, 24

captive breeding, 23–24
color, 4, 6–7, 10

dens, 5, 6
development, 17–18, 22,
    23
diseases, 12–13, 26–27

education, 6, 26
endangered species, 5, 6,
    14, 16, 20, 26
Everglades, 5, 27
eyes, 4, 6–7

Fakahatchee Strand State
    Preserve, 21
females, 4, 5, 8, 10, 11,
    23, 24
fighting, 8, 12
Florida Game and
    Freshwater Fish
    Commission, 16
Florida Panther National
    Wildlife Refuge, 21
Florida Panther Refuge, 6
Florida Panther Society, 26
Florida Panther Trust Fund, 24

food, 5–6, 7, 11, 15,
    23, 28
fur, 4, 10, 19

gene pools, 18–19, 23,
    24
governments, 5, 16, 21,
    22, 28

habitat, 5, 6, 8, 9–10,
    14, 16, 18, 21–22,
    23, 24, 25–26, 29
humans, 5, 6, 13, 15–17,
    23, 27, 28
hunting, 6, 7, 15

kittens, 4–5, 6–7, 8, 19,
    24

legs, 10
length, 10, 11
lifespan, 12

males, 8, 10, 12
mating, 8, 19, 23–24
milk, 5, 6

Native Americans, 15

pets, 23, 27
population, 8, 13, 21, 24,
    25–26

predators, 11
prey, 6, 7, 11, 15, 23,
    28
Puma concolor family, 9

radio collars, 13, 27
Recovery Team, 26
reintroduction, 22–23
roadways, 13, 17, 24,
    27, 28

size, 10–11
Species Survival Plan,
    20–21, 22
subspecies, 9, 14

tails, 4, 6, 19
territory, 5, 6, 8, 12, 27
Texas cougars, 24

umbrella species, 16

vaccines, 12–13
vehicle collisions, 13,
    27–28

weight, 4–5, 10–11
wetlands, 5, 17–18,
    21–22, 27

ABOUT THE AUTHOR

Barbara A. Somervill writes children's nonfiction books on a variety of topics. She is particularly interested in nature and foreign countries. Somervill believes that researching new and different topics makes writing every book an adventure. When she is not writing, she is an avid reader and plays bridge.